This book belongs to

_____

Happy Like Me

Phyllis Larson

Order this book online at www.trafford.com
or email orders@trafford.com

Most Trafford titles are also available at major online book retailers.

© Copyright 2009 Phyllis Larson.
Illustrated by Pamela Edevold.

All rights reserved. No part of this publication may be reproduced, stored in a retrieval system, or transmitted, in any form or by any means, electronic, mechanical, photocopying, recording, or otherwise, without the written prior permission of the author.

Printed in the United States of America.

ISBN: 978-1-4269-3138-3

Library of Congress Control Number: 2010905023

Our mission is to efficiently provide the world's finest, most comprehensive book publishing service, enabling every author to experience success. To find out how to publish your book, your way, and have it available worldwide, visit us online at www.trafford.com

Trafford rev. 4/30/2010

 www.trafford.com

North America & international
toll-free: 1 888 232 4444 (USA & Canada)
phone: 250 383 6864 • fax: 812 355 4082

"This book is dedicated to children everywhere. Each one is blessed with unique beauty and innocence that only a child can possess.

Lift me up, Papa! I want to see myself in your sparkly eyes. I like to play with your whiskery face. One of my most favorite places to be is way up high in my Papa's arms.
That really makes me happy.

I like to spend all day playing in the trees.
The squirrels and the birds don't seem to mind.
We laugh and climb and swing like monkeys.
That really makes me happy.

Honking trucks and tooting trains are my favorite toys. Sorry! No girls allowed, only boys today! Mommy says my friend can sleep over with me. That really makes me happy.

These are my very special friends.
Here is my really big, stuffed doggy and my little stuffed puppies, my soft squishy tiger and my fuzzy brown bear. Rickee, my raccoon, wants to play with my dolly and me.
That really makes me happy.

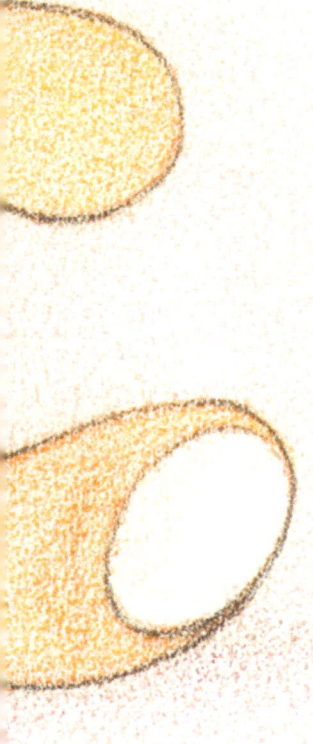

Oh, thank you Mommy and Daddy, for our brand new baby brother! He is so cute. He makes a funny, crookedly smile when he looks up at my sister and me.
That really makes me happy.

Keep twirling! Keep twirling! I know I can do it!
This hoop is kind of big for a little girl like me.
I'm so lucky, because I get to hula hoop
with the big girls!
That really makes me happy.

Go faster, Grammy! Go faster!
Be careful, we don't want to fall.
Oh! Oh! We're starting to get kind of tipsy!
I like three-legged racing with my Grammy.
That really makes me happy.

Giddyup, horse! Giddyup!
Be careful, don't step on my doggie!
I'll hang on tight to the saddle and you
hang on tight to me. Together, we will ride
way up high in the sky!
That really makes me happy.

Look at that funny clown!
The monkeys sure got him wet!
It's fun to go to the circus,
especially when you can go with me.
That really makes me happy.

I'm all tucked in, snuggly in my bed.
I kissed everyone goodnight and I said my prayers.
I know I'll be safe as I sleep tight,
because God always sends a beautiful angel
to stay with me all night.
That really makes me happy.